To Ann, who can out-hug a Bumbletum
—S.S.

For the kids—Fluff, Kangaroo,
and the Mole Brothers, *et al.*
—T.W.

tiger tales
an imprint of ME Media, LLC
202 Old Ridgefield Road, Wilton, CT 06897
Published in the United States 2006
Originally published in Great Britain 2006
By Little Tiger Press
An imprint of Magi Publications
Text copyright ©2006 Steve Smallman
Illustrations copyright ©2006 Tim Warnes
CIP data is available
ISBN-13: 978-1-58925-060-4
ISBN-10: 1-58925-060-5
Printed in Singapore
1 3 5 7 9 10 8 6 4 2

Bumbletum

by Steve Smallman

Illustrated by Tim Warnes

tiger tales

There was a new toy in the bedroom. He was small, soft, and floppy, and he had a squishy tummy covered in stripes.

His name was Bumbletum.

"Hello," said Milly Mouse.
"What kind of toy are you?"
Bumbletum thought
very hard and then said,
"This kind."

"And what can you do?" asked Teddy Bear.

Bumbletum thought even harder. "Something good," he said. "But I don't know what it is yet."

"We'll help you figure it out!" said the toys.

"You look like a mouse," said Milly. "Can you squeak like this?"

SQUEAK!
SQUEAK!

Bumbletum tried and Milly
helped, but nothing happened.

Bumbletum tried and
Teddy helped, but
nothing happened.

"Your tail is kind of like mine," said Peter Puppy. "Can you wag it like this?"

WIGGLE WAGGLE!

WIGGLE WAGGLE!

Bumbletum tried,
but instead of wiggling
and waggling, he wibbled
and wobbled . . .

and fell over.

Then another toy came over. It was Baby Drink and Wet.

"Can you wet yourself like this?" she asked, and she made a little puddle.

TINKLE
TINKLE!

Bumbletum was impressed.
He tried and tried and tried,
but nothing happened.

Worn out, Bumbletum flopped down on the floor.

"I must be a 'doesn't really do anything' kind of toy," he said quietly.

But the others were sure there was something Bumbletum could do.

"I know!" cried Boomer Kangaroo, bouncing over. "It's your tummy!"

"My tummy?" asked Bumbletum.

"It's striped like a bumblebee, and what can bumblebees do?"

"Buzz?" asked Bumbletum.

"FLY!" said Boomer, and the others agreed.

Milly and Boomer helped
Bumbletum up on to the bed.
"When you're ready, JUMP!"
the toys shouted.

But Bumbletum wasn't ready. The bed was very high and the floor was a very long way down. His knees started to shake and his tummy felt funny.

"I'M NOT A BEE!" he cried. "I DON'T THINK I'M SUPPOSED TO FLY!"

"Try bouncing first, like this!" Boomer said. Then Milly joined in. They bounced up and down, up and down, higher and higher.

BOING!

BOING!

"LOOK, BUMBLETUM!
I'M FLYING!" Milly squeaked,
but then . . .

Milly fell off the bed!

"DON'T WORRY, MILLY! I'M COMING!" Bumbletum called. He slid down the quilt to land FLUMP on the floor.

He scooped Milly up in his arms and gave her a BIG hug.

Bumbletum's tummy was so soft and snuggly that Milly felt better right away, but she stayed a bit longer just to be sure.

"Thank you, Bumbletum," she said. "That's the best hug I've ever had!"

"HUGGING!" Bumbletum cried. "THAT'S WHAT I CAN DO! Who wants a hug?"

The toys all ran over and settled down in a cozy heap with Bumbletum right in the middle. He knew then that being a Bumbletum was very, very special indeed!

WIGGLE WAGGLE!